FATAL INTERVIEW

"*By our first strange and fatall interview,*
By all desires which thereof did ensue"
—JOHN DONNE

Fatal Interview

Sonnets

BY

EDNA ST. VINCENT MILLAY

HARPER & BROTHERS *Publishers*
New York *and* London
MCMXXXI

OTHER BOOKS BY
EDNA ST. VINCENT MILLAY

———

THE LAMP AND THE BELL
SECOND APRIL
THREE PLAYS
RENASCENCE
A FEW FIGS FROM THISTLES
THE HARP-WEAVER
ARIA DA CAPO
THE KING'S HENCHMAN
THE BUCK IN THE SNOW

———

Harper & Brothers
Publishers

TO

ELINOR WYLIE

When I think of you,
I die, too.
In my throat, bereft
Like yours, of air,
No sound is left,
Nothing is there
To make a word of grief.

CONTENTS

x

FATAL INTERVIEW

Fatal Interview

I

WHAT thing is this that, built of salt and lime
And such dry motes as in the sunbeam show,
Has power upon me that do daily climb
The dustless air?—for whom those peaks of snow
Whereup the lungs of man with borrowed breath
Go labouring to a doom I may not feel,
Are but a pearled and roseate plain beneath
My wingèd helmet and my wingèd heel.
What sweet emotions neither foe nor friend
Are these that clog my flight? what thing is this
That hastening headlong to a dusty end
Dare turn upon me these proud eyes of bliss?
Up, up, my feathers!—ere I lay you by
To journey barefoot with a mortal joy.

II

This beast that rends me in the sight of all,
This love, this longing, this oblivious thing,
That has me under as the last leaves fall,
Will glut, will sicken, will be gone by spring.
The wound will heal, the fever will abate,
The knotted hurt will slacken in the breast;
I shall forget before the flickers mate
Your look that is today my east and west.
Unscathed, however, from a claw so deep
Though I should love again I shall not go:
Along my body, waking while I sleep,
Sharp to the kiss, cold to the hand as snow,
The scar of this encounter like a sword
Will lie between me and my troubled lord.

III

No LACK of counsel from the shrewd and wise
How love may be acquired and how conserved
Warrants this laying bare before your eyes
My needle to your north abruptly swerved;
If I would hold you, I must hide my fears
Lest you be wanton, lead you to believe
My compass to another quarter veers,
Little surrender, lavishly receive.
But being like my mother the brown earth
Fervent and full of gifts and free from guile,
Liefer would I you loved me for my worth,
Though you should love me but a little while,
Than for a philtre any doll can brew,—
Though thus I bound you as I long to do.

IV "

Nay, learnèd doctor, these fine leeches fresh
From the pond's edge my cause cannot remove:
Alas, the sick disorder in my flesh
Is deeper than your skill, is very love.
And you, good friar, far liefer would I think
Upon my dear, and dream him in your place,
Than heed your *ben'cites* and heavenward sink
With empty heart and noddle full of grace.
Breathes but one mortal on the teeming globe
Could minister to my soul's or body's needs—
Physician minus physic, minus robe;
Confessor minus Latin, minus beads.
Yet should you bid me name him, I am dumb;
For though you summon him, he would not come.

V"

Of all that ever in extreme disease
"Sweet Love, sweet cruel Love, have pity!" cried,
Count me the humblest, hold me least of these
That wear the red heart crumpled in the side,
In heaviest durance, dreaming or awake,
Filling the dungeon with their piteous woe;
Not that I shriek not till the dungeon shake,
"Oh, God! Oh, let me out! Oh, let me go!"
But that my chains throughout their iron length
Make such a golden clank upon my ear,
But that I would not, boasted I the strength,
Up with a terrible arm and out of here
Where thrusts my morsel daily through the bars
This tall, oblivious gaoler eyed with stars.

SINCE I cannot persuade you from this mood
Of pale preoccupation with the dead,
Not for my comfort nor for your own good
Shift your concern to living bones instead;
Since that which Helen did and ended Troy
Is more than I can do though I be warm,
Have up your buried girls, egregious boy,
And stand with them against the unburied storm.
When you lie wasted and your blood runs thin,
And what's to do must with dispatch be done,
Call Cressid, call Elaine, call Isolt in!—
More bland the ichor of a ghost should run
Along your dubious veins than the rude sea
Of passion pounding all day long in me.

VII

Night is my sister, and how deep in love,
How drowned in love and weedily washed ashore,
There to be fretted by the drag and shove
At the tide's edge, I lie—these things and more:
Whose arm alone between me and the sand,
Whose voice alone, whose pitiful breath brought near,
Could thaw these nostrils and unlock this hand,
She could advise you, should you care to hear.
Small chance, however, in a storm so black,
A man will leave his friendly fire and snug
For a drowned woman's sake, and bring her back
To drip and scatter shells upon the rug.
No one but Night, with tears on her dark face,
Watches beside me in this windy place.

VIII

Yet in an hour to come, disdainful dust,
You shall be bowed and brought to bed with me.
While the blood roars, or when the blood is rust
About a broken engine, this shall be.
If not today, then later; if not here
On the green grass, with sighing and delight,
Then under it, all in good time, my dear,
We shall be laid together in the night.
And ruder and more violent, be assured,
Than the desirous body's heat and sweat
That shameful kiss by more than night obscured
Wherewith at length the scornfullest mouth is met.
Life has no friend; her converts late or soon
Slide back to feed the dragon with the moon.

IX

Wʜᴇɴ you are dead, and your disturbing eyes
No more as now their stormy lashes lift
To lance me through—as in the morning skies
One moment, plainly visible in a rift
Of cloud, two splendid planets may appear
And purely blaze, and are at once withdrawn,
What time the watcher in desire and fear
Leans from his chilly window in the dawn—
Shall I be free, shall I be once again
As others are, and count your loss no care?
Oh, never more, till my dissolving brain
Be powerless to evoke you out of air,
Remembered morning stars, more fiercely bright
Than all the Alphas of the actual night!

X

STRANGE thing that I, by nature nothing prone
To fret the summer blossom on its stem,
Who know the hidden nest, but leave alone
The magic eggs, the bird that cuddles them,
Should have no peace till your bewildered heart
Hung fluttering at the window of my breast,
Till I had ravished to my bitter smart
Your kiss from the stern moment, could not rest.
"Swift wing, sweet blossom, live again in air!
Depart, poor flower; poor feathers you are free!"
Thus do I cry, being teased by shame and care
That beauty should be brought to terms by me;
Yet shamed the more that in my heart I know,
Cry as I may, I could not let you go.

Not in a silver casket cool with pearls
Or rich with red corundum or with blue,
Locked, and the key withheld, as other girls
Have given their loves, I give my love to you;
Not in a lovers'-knot, not in a ring
Worked in such fashion, and the legend plain—
Semper fidelis, where a secret spring
Kennels a drop of mischief for the brain:
Love in the open hand, no thing but that,
Ungemmed, unhidden, wishing not to hurt,
As one should bring you cowslips in a hat
Swung from the hand, or apples in her skirt,
I bring you, calling out as children do:
"Look what I have!—And these are all for you."

XII

Olympian gods, mark now my bedside lamp
Blown out; and be advised too late that he
Whom you call sire is stolen into the camp
Of warring Earth, and lies abed with me.
Call out your golden hordes, the harm is done:
Enraptured in his great embrace I lie;
Shake heaven with spears, but I shall bear a son
Branded with godhead, heel and brow and thigh.
Whom think not to bedazzle or confound
With meteoric splendours or display
Of blackened moons or suns or the big sound
Of sudden thunder on a silent day;
Pain and compassion shall he know, being mine,—
Confusion never, that is half divine.

XIII

I SAID, seeing how the winter gale increased,
Even as waxed within us and grew strong
The ancient tempest of desire, "At least,
It is the season when the nights are long.
Well flown, well shattered from the summer hedge
The early sparrow and the opening flowers!—
Late climbs the sun above the southerly edge
These days, and sweet to love those added hours."
Alas, already does the dark recede,
And visible are the trees against the snow.
Oh, monstrous parting, oh, perfidious deed,
How shall I leave your side, how shall I go? . . .
Unnatural night, the shortest of the year,
Farewell! 'Tis dawn. The longest day is here.

XIV

Since of no creature living the last breath
Is twice required, or twice the ultimate pain,
Seeing how to quit your arms is very death,
'Tis likely that I shall not die again;
And likely 'tis that Time whose gross decree
Sends now the dawn to clamour at our door,
Thus having done his evil worst to me,
Will thrust me by, will harry me no more.
When you are corn and roses and at rest
I shall endure, a dense and sanguine ghost,
To haunt the scene where I was happiest,
To bend above the thing I loved the most;
And rise, and wring my hands, and steal away
As I do now, before the advancing day.

XV

My worship from this hour the Sparrow-Drawn
Alone will cherish, and her arrowy child,
Whose groves alone in the inquiring dawn
Rise tranquil, and their altars undefiled.
Seaward and shoreward smokes a plundered land
To guard whose portals was my dear employ;
Razed are its temples now; inviolate stand
Only the slopes of Venus and her boy.
How have I stripped me of immortal aid
Save theirs alone,—who could endure to see
Forsworn Aeneas with conspiring blade
Sever the ship from shore (alas for me)
And make no sign; who saw, and did not speak,
The brooch of Troilus pinned upon the Greek.

I DREAMED I moved among the Elysian fields,
In converse with sweet women long since dead;
And out of blossoms which that meadow yields
I wove a garland for your living head.
Danae, that was the vessel for a day
Of golden Jove, I saw, and at her side,
Whom Jove the Bull desired and bore away,
Europa stood, and the Swan's featherless bride.
All these were mortal women, yet all these
Above the ground had had a god for guest;
Freely I walked beside them and at ease,
Addressing them, by them again addressed,
And marvelled nothing, for remembering you,
Wherefore I was among them well I knew.

XVII

Sweet love, sweet thorn, when lightly to my heart
I took your thrust, whereby I since am slain,
And lie disheveled in the grass apart,
A sodden thing bedrenched by tears and rain,
While rainy evening drips to misty night,
And misty night to cloudy morning clears,
And clouds disperse across the gathering light,
And birds grow noisy, and the sun appears—
Had I bethought me then, sweet love, sweet thorn,
How sharp an anguish even at the best—
When all's requited and the future sworn—
The happy hour can leave within the breast,
I had not so come running at the call
Of one who loves me little, if at all.

XVIII

SHALL I be prisoner till my pulses stop
To hateful Love and drag his noisy chain,
And bait my need with sugared crusts that drop
From jeweled fingers neither kind nor clean?—
Mewed in an airless cavern where a toad
Would grieve to snap his gnat and lay him down,
While in the light along the rattling road
Men shout and chaff and drive their wares to town?...
Perfidious Prince, that keep me here confined,
Doubt not I know the letters of my doom:
How many a man has left his blood behind
To buy his exit from this mournful room
These evil stains record, these walls that rise
Carved with his torment, steamy with his sighs.

XIX

My most distinguished guest and learnèd friend,
The pallid hare that runs before the day
Having brought your earnest counsels to an end
Now have I somewhat of my own to say:
That it is folly to be sunk in love,
And madness plain to make the matter known,
These are no mysteries you are verger of;
Everyman's wisdoms these are, and my own.
If I have flung my heart unto a hound
I have done ill, it is a certain thing;
Yet breathe I freer, walk I the more sound
On my sick bones for this brave reasoning?
Soon must I say, "'Tis prowling Death I hear!"—
Yet come no better off, for my quick ear.

XX

THINK not, nor for a moment let your mind,
Wearied with thinking, doze upon the thought
That the work's done and the long day behind,
And beauty, since 'tis paid for, can be bought.
If in the moonlight from the silent bough
Suddenly with precision speak your name
The nightingale, be not assured that now
His wing is limed and his wild virtue tame.
Beauty beyond all feathers that have flown
Is free; you shall not hood her to your wrist,
Nor sting her eyes, nor have her for your own
In any fashion; beauty billed and kissed
Is not your turtle; tread her like a dove—
She loves you not; she never heard of love.

EIGHT

important

Modern Poets

HARPER &
BROTHERS

Edna St. Vincent Millay

FATAL INTERVIEW

A new volume of love sonnets, Miss Millay's most recent work.

THE BUCK IN THE SNOW

"Of this golden collection it is impossible to stint praise. Conveyed with surpassing delicacy of beauty."—*Percy Hutchinson, New York Times Book Review.*

A FEW FIGS FROM THISTLES

"She has a wayward faery quality, and, more than any other American poet, a certain kind of magnificence."—*New York Herald Tribune.*

THE HARP WEAVER

"Far and away the finest book of poems of the year—yes, and of many other years too."—*John V. A. Weaver.*

RENASCENCE

"One of the loveliest of American poems. If it has the movement of a bird's flight, it has the ease of a bird's song."—*Carl Van Doren.*

SECOND APRIL

"She does not play with words; she plays them, as the notes of an instrument; and with equal command and effect moves them up and down, runs them out to an ode, or contracts them to an epigram."—*Manchester Guardian.*

THE KING'S HENCHMAN

"A beautiful thing, which delicately lifts the stark life of our forebears into the purest atmosphere of romance."—*Atlantic Monthly.*

The above volumes in cloth—$2.00. In Leather—$3.00.

ARIA DA CAPO, *a Play*	Cloth $2.00
THE LAMP AND THE BELL, *a Play*	Cloth $2.00
THREE PLAYS	Cloth $2.00
SELECTED POEMS FOR YOUNG PEOPLE	Cloth $2.50

Countee Cullen

THE BLACK CHRIST

"Beauty of imagery, vigor of line and intensity of mood are sustained throughout."—*Granville Hicks, New York World.* $2.00

COLOR

"Few books of poems have been so tuneful, at least so tuneful in the execution of significant themes."—*The World Tomorrow.* $2.00

COPPER SUN

"Fifty-eight poems, charming, versatile, and satisfying." —*The World Tomorrow.* $2.00

BALLAD OF THE BROWN GIRL

"A poem worth knowing, in a book worth possessing."— *Boston Transcript.* $2.00

Roy Helton

LONESOME WATER

"A book of singing words, of deep quiet places, of sweet water and sunlight, of love, of quaint old thoughts and windy hills."—*Philadelphia Public Ledger.* $2.00

Edward Davison

HARVEST OF YOUTH

"He writes with a freshness and spontaneity which is all the more appealing because it flows so melodiously and simply."—*Springfield Republican.* $2.00

Christy MacKaye

WIND IN THE GRASS

"I find the presence of something for which there is no name in the dictionaries . . . a quality unusual and untangible . . . a real imagination."—*Edwin Arlington Robinson in his Introductory Letter.* $2.00

Joseph Auslander

LETTERS TO WOMEN
"Uncommonly good, both as poetry and as sagacious comment."—*New York Times*. $2.00

SUNRISE TRUMPETS $2.00

CYCLOPS' EYE $2.00

Elizabeth Hollister Frost

HOVERING SHADOW
"Subjective and emotional; good in its technique, in its lyric quality, in its content."—*Boston Transcript*. $2.00

THE LOST LYRIST $2.00

Edmund Blunden

NEAR AND FAR
"It has dignity, excellent craftsmanship, a fortitude in relation to life, a tenderness toward beauty."—*Philadelphia Public Ledger*. $2.00

Order Form

TO YOUR BOOKSELLER:

Please send me the books I have checked in this circular:

☐ Remittance enclosed. ☐ C.O.D. ☐ Charge my account.

Name ....

Street ....

City and State ....

XXI

Gone in good sooth you are: not even in dream
You come. As if the strictures of the light,
Laid on our glances to their disesteem,
Extended even to shadows and the night;
Extended even beyond that drowsy sill
Along whose galleries open to the skies
All maskers move unchallenged and at will,
Visor in hand or hooded to the eyes.
To that pavilion the green sea in flood
Curves in, and the slow dancers dance in foam;
I find again the pink camellia-bud
On the wide step, beside a silver comb. . . .
But it is scentless; up the marble stair
I mount with pain, knowing you are not there.

XXII

Now by this moon, before this moon shall wane
I shall be dead or I shall be with you!
No moral concept can outweigh the pain
Past rack and wheel this absence puts me through;
Faith, honour, pride, endurance, what the tongues
Of tedious men will say, or what the law—
For which of these do I fill up my lungs
With brine and fire at every breath I draw?
Time, and to spare, for patience by and by,
Time to be cold and time to sleep alone;
Let me no more until the hour I die
Defraud my innocent senses of their own.
Before this moon shall darken, say of me:
She's in her grave, or where she wants to be.

XXIII

I KNOW the face of Falsehood and her tongue
Honeyed with unction, plausible with guile,
Are dear to men, whom count me not among,
That owe their daily credit to her smile;
Such have been succoured out of great distress
By her contriving, if accounts be true:
Their deference now above the board, I guess,
Discharges what beneath the board is due.
As for myself, I'd liefer lack her aid
Than eat her presence; let this building fall,
But let me never lift my latch, afraid
To hear her simpering accents in the hall,
Nor force an entrance past mephitic airs
Of stale patchouli hanging on my stairs.

XXIV

WHEREAS at morning in a jeweled crown
I bit my fingers and was hard to please,
Having shook disaster till the fruit fell down
I feel tonight more happy and at ease;
Feet running in the corridors, men quick-
Buckling their sword-belts bumping down the stair,
Challenge, and rattling bridge-chain, and the click
Of hooves on pavement—this will clear the air.
Private this chamber as it has not been
In many a month of muffled hours; almost,
Lulled by the uproar, I could lie serene
And sleep, until all's won, until all's lost,
And the door's opened and the issue shown,
And I walk forth Hell's mistress . . . or my own.

XXV

PERIL upon the paths of this desire
Lies like the natural darkness of the night,
For me unpeopled; let him hence retire
Whom as a child a shadow could affright;
And fortune speed him from this dubious place
Where roses blenched or blackened of their hue,
Pallid and stemless float on undulant space,
Or clustered hidden shock the hand with dew.
Whom as a child the night's obscurity
Did not alarm, let him alone remain,
Lanterned but by the longing in the eye,
And warmed but by the fever in the vein,
To lie with me, sentried from wrath and scorn
By sleepless Beauty and her polished thorn.

XXVI

Women have loved before as I love now;
At least, in lively chronicles of the past—
Of Irish waters by a Cornish prow
Or Trojan waters by a Spartan mast
Much to their cost invaded—here and there,
Hunting the amorous line, skimming the rest,
I find some woman bearing as I bear
Love like a burning city in the breast.
I think however that of all alive
I only in such utter, ancient way
Do suffer love; in me alone survive
The unregenerate passions of a day
When treacherous queens, with death upon the tread,
Heedless and wilful, took their knights to bed.

XXVII

Moon, that against the lintel of the west
Your forehead lean until the gate be swung,
Longing to leave the world and be at rest,
Being worn with faring and no longer young,
Do you recall at all the Carian hill
Where worn with loving, loving late you lay,
Halting the sun because you lingered still,
While wondering candles lit the Carian day?
Ah, if indeed this memory to your mind
Recall some sweet employment, pity me,
That with the dawn must leave my love behind,
That even now the dawn's dim herald see!
I charge you, goddess, in the name of one
You loved as well: endure, hold off the sun.

XXVIII

WHEN we are old and these rejoicing veins
Are frosty channels to a muted stream,
And out of all our burning there remains
No feeblest spark to fire us, even in dream,
This be our solace: that it was not said
When we were young and warm and in our prime,
Upon our couch we lay as lie the dead,
Sleeping away the unreturning time.
O sweet, O heavy-lidded, O my love,
When morning strikes her spear upon the land,
And we must rise and arm us and reprove
The insolent daylight with a steady hand,
Be not discountenanced if the knowing know
We rose from rapture but an hour ago.

XXIX

Heart, have no pity on this house of bone:
Shake it with dancing, break it down with joy.
No man holds mortgage on it; it is your own;
To give, to sell at auction, to destroy.
When you are blind to moonlight on the bed,
When you are deaf to gravel on the pane,
Shall quavering caution from this house instead
Cluck forth at summer mischief in the lane?
All that delightful youth forbears to spend
Molestful age inherits, and the ground
Will have us; therefore, while we're young, my friend—
The Latin's vulgar, but the advice is sound.
Youth, have no pity; leave no farthing here
For age to invest in compromise and fear.

XXX

LOVE is not all; it is not meat nor drink
Nor slumber nor a roof against the rain,
Nor yet a floating spar to men that sink
And rise and sink and rise and sink again;
Love can not fill the thickened lung with breath,
Nor clean the blood, nor set the fractured bone;
Yet many a man is making friends with death
Even as I speak, for lack of love alone.
It well may be that in a difficult hour,
Pinned down by pain and moaning for release,
Or nagged by want past resolution's power,
I might be driven to sell your love for peace,
Or trade the memory of this night for food.
It well may be. I do not think I would.

XXXI

WHEN we that wore the myrtle wear the dust,
And years of darkness cover up our eyes,
And all our arrogant laughter and sweet lust
Keep counsel with the scruples of the wise;
When boys and girls that now are in the loins
Of croaking lads, dip oar into the sea,—
And who are these that dive for copper coins?
No longer we, my love, no longer we—
Then let the fortunate breathers of the air,
When we lie speechless in the muffling mould,
Tease not our ghosts with slander, pause not there
To say that love is false and soon grows cold,
But pass in silence the mute grave of two
Who lived and died believing love was true.

XXXII

Time, that is pleased to lengthen out the day
For grieving lovers parted or denied,
And pleased to hurry the sweet hours away
From such as lie enchanted side by side,
Is not my kinsman; nay, my feudal foe
Is he that in my childhood was the thief
Of all my mother's beauty, and in woe
My father bowed, and brought our house to grief.
Thus, though he think to touch with hateful frost
Your treasured curls, and your clear forehead line,
And so persuade me from you, he has lost;
Never shall he inherit what was mine.
When Time and all his tricks have done their worst,
Still will I hold you dear, and him accurst.

XXXIII

Sorrowful dreams remembered after waking
Shadow with dolour all the candid day;
Even as I read, the silly tears out-breaking
Splash on my hands and shut the page away. . . .
Grief at the root, a dark and secret dolour,
Harder to bear than wind-and-weather grief,
Clutching the rose, draining its cheek of colour,
Drying the bud, curling the opened leaf.
Deep is the pond—although the edge be shallow,
Frank in the sun, revealing fish and stone,
Climbing ashore to turtle-head and mallow—
Black at the centre beats a heart unknown.
Desolate dreams pursue me out of sleep;
Weeping I wake; waking, I weep, I weep.

XXXIV

Most wicked words, forbear to speak them out.
Utter them not again. Blaspheme no more
Against our love with maxims learned from Doubt,
Lest Death should get his foot inside the door.
We are surrounded by a hundred foes;
And he that at your bidding joins our feast,
I stake my heart upon it, is one of those,
Nor in their councils does he sit the least.
Hark not his whisper; he is Time's ally,
Kinsman to Death and leman of Despair.
Believe that I shall love you till I die;
Believe, and thrust him forth, and arm the stair,
And top the walls with spikes and splintered glass,
That he pass gutted, should again he pass.

XXXV

CLEARLY my ruined garden as it stood
Before the frost came on it I recall—
Stiff marigolds, and what a trunk of wood
The zinnia had, that was the first to fall;
These pale and oozy stalks, these hanging leaves
Nerveless and darkened, dripping in the sun,
Cannot gainsay me, though the spirit grieves
And wrings its hands at what the frost has done.
If in a widening silence you should guess
I read the moment with recording eyes,
Taking your love and all your loveliness
Into a listening body hushed of sighs,
Though summer's rife and the warm rose in season,
Rebuke me not: I have a winter reason.

XXXVI

Hearing your words, and not a word among them
Tuned to my liking, on a salty day
When inland woods were pushed by winds that flung
    them
Hissing to leeward like a ton of spray,
I thought how off Matinicus the tide
Came pounding in, came running through the Gut,
While from the Rock the warning whistle cried,
And children whimpered, and the doors blew shut;
There in the autumn when the men go forth,
With slapping skirts the island women stand
In gardens stripped and scattered, peering north,
With dahlia tubers dripping from the hand:
The wind of their endurance, driving south,
Flattened your words against your speaking mouth.

XXXVII

BELIEVE, if ever the bridges of this town,
Whose towers were builded without fault or stain,
Be taken, and its battlements go down,
No mortal roof shall shelter me again;
I shall not prop a branch against a bough
To hide me from the whipping east or north,
Nor tease to flame a heap of sticks, that now
Am warmed by all the wonders of the earth.
Do you take ship unto some happier shore
In such event, and have no thought for me.
I shall remain;—to share the ruinous floor
With roofs that once were seen far out at sea;
To cheer a mouldering army on the march,
And beg from spectres by a broken arch.

XXXVIII

You say: "Since life is cruel enough at best,"
You say: "Considering how our love is cursed,
And housed so bleakly that the sea-gull's nest
Were better shelter, even as better nursed
Between the breaker and the stingy reeds
Ragged and coarse that hiss against the sand
The gull's brown chick, and hushed in all his needs,
Than our poor love so harried through the land—
You being too tender, even with all your scorn,
To line his cradle with the world's reproof,
And I too devious, too surrendered, born
Too far from home to hunt him even a roof
Out of the rain—" Oh, tortured voice, be still!
Spare me your premise: leave me when you will.

XXXIX

Love me no more, now let the god depart,
If love be grown so bitter to your tongue!
Here is my hand; I bid you from my heart
Fare well, fare very well, be always young.
As for myself, mine was a deeper drouth,
I drank and thirsted still; but I surmise
My kisses now are sand against your mouth,
Teeth in your palm and pennies on your eyes.
Speak but one cruel word, to shame my tears;
Go, but in going, stiffen up my back
To meet the yelping of the mustering years—
Dim, trotting shapes that seldom will attack
Two with a light who match their steps and sing:
To one alone and lost, another thing.

XL

You loved me not at all, but let it go;
I loved you more than life, but let it be.
As the more injured party, this being so,
The hour's amenities are all to me—
The choice of weapons; and I gravely choose
To let the weapons tarnish where they lie,
And spend the night in eloquent abuse
Of senators and popes and such small fry
And meet the morning standing, and at odds
With heaven and earth and hell and any fool
That calls his soul his own, and all the gods,
And all the children getting dressed for school . . .
And you will leave me, and I shall entomb
What's cold by then in an adjoining room.

XLI

I said in the beginning, did I not?—
Prophetic of the end, though unaware
How light you took me, ignorant that you thought
I spoke to see my breath upon the air:
If you walk east at daybreak from the town
To the cliff's foot, by climbing steadily
You cling at noon whence there is no way down
But to go toppling backward to the sea.
And not for birds nor birds'-eggs, so they say,
But for a flower that in these fissures grows,
Forms have been seen to move throughout the day
Skyward; but what its name is no one knows.
'Tis said you find beside them on the sand
This flower, relinquished by the broken hand.

XLII

O AILING Love, compose your struggling wing!
Confess you mortal; be content to die.
How better dead, than be this awkward thing
Dragging in dust its feathers of the sky,
Hitching and rearing, plunging beak to loam,
Upturned, disheveled, utt'ring a weak sound
Less proud than of the gull that rakes the foam,
Less kind than of the hawk that scours the ground.
While yet your awful beauty, even at bay,
Beats off the impious eye, the outstretched hand,
And what your hue or fashion none can say,
Vanish, be fled, leave me a wingless land . . .
Save where one moment down the quiet tide
Fades a white swan, with a black swan beside.

XLIII

Summer, be seen no more within this wood;
Nor you, red Autumn, down its paths appear;
Let no more the false mitrewort intrude
Nor the dwarf cornel nor the gentian here;
You too be absent, unavailing Spring,
Nor let those thrushes that with pain conspire
From out this wood their wild arpeggios fling,
Shaking the nerves with memory and desire.
Only that season which is no man's friend,
You, surly Winter, in this wood be found;
Freeze up the year; with sleet these branches bend
Though rasps the locust in the fields around.
Now darken, sky! Now shrieking blizzard, blow!—
Farewell, sweet bank; be blotted out with snow.

XLIV

If to be left were to be left alone,
And lock the door and find one's self again—
Drag forth and dust Penates of one's own
That in a corner all too long have lain;
Read Brahms, read Chaucer, set the chessmen out
In classic problem, stretch the shrunken mind
Back to its stature on the rack of thought—
Loss might be said to leave its boon behind.
But fruitless conference and the interchange
With callow wits of bearded *cons* and *pros*
Enlist the neutral daylight, and derange
A will too sick to battle for repose.
Neither with you nor with myself, I spend
Loud days that have no meaning and no end.

XLV

I KNOW my mind and I have made my choice;
Not from your temper does my doom depend;
Love me or love me not, you have no voice
In this, that is my portion to the end.
Your presence and your favours, the full part
That you could give, you now can take away:
What lies between your beauty and my heart
Not even you can trouble or betray.
Mistake me not—unto my inmost core
I do desire your kiss upon my mouth;
They have not craved a cup of water more
That bleach upon the deserts of the south;
Here might you bless me; what you cannot do
Is bow me down, that have been loved by you.

XLVI

Even in the moment of our earliest kiss,
When sighed the straitened bud into the flower,
Sat the dry seed of most unwelcome this;
And that I knew, though not the day and hour.
Too season-wise am I, being country-bred,
To tilt at autumn or defy the frost:
Snuffing the chill even as my fathers did,
I say with them, "What's out tonight is lost."
I only hoped, with the mild hope of all
Who watch the leaf take shape upon the tree,
A fairer summer and a later fall
Than in these parts a man is apt to see,
And sunny clusters ripened for the wine:
I tell you this across the blackened vine.

XLVII

WELL, I have lost you; and I lost you fairly;
In my own way, and with my full consent.
Say what you will, kings in a tumbrel rarely
Went to their deaths more proud that this one went.
Some nights of apprehension and hot weeping
I will confess; but that's permitted me;
Day dried my eyes; I was not one for keeping
Rubbed in a cage a wing that would be free.
If I had loved you less or played you slyly
I might have held you for a summer more,
But at the cost of words I value highly,
And no such summer as the one before.
Should I outlive this anguish—and men do—
I shall have only good to say of you.

XLVIII

Now by the path I climbed, I journey back.
The oaks have grown; I have been long away.
Taking with me your memory and your lack
I now descend into a milder day;
Stripped of your love, unburdened of my hope,
Descend the path I mounted from the plain;
Yet steeper than I fancied seems the slope
And stonier, now that I go down again.
Warm falls the dusk; the clanking of a bell
Faintly ascends upon this heavier air;
I do recall those grassy pastures well:
In early spring they drove the cattle there.
And close at hand should be a shelter, too,
From which the mountain peaks are not in view.

XLIX

There is a well into whose bottomless eye,
Though I were flayed, I dare not lean and look,
Sweet once with mountain water, now gone dry,
Miraculously abandoned by the brook
Wherewith for years miraculously fed
It kept a constant level cold and bright,
Though summer parched the rivers in their bed;
Withdrawn these waters, vanished overnight.
There is a word I dare not speak again,
A face I never again must call to mind;
I was not craven ever nor blenched at pain,
But pain to such degree and of such kind
As I must suffer if I think of you,
Not in my senses will I undergo.

L

THE heart once broken is a heart no more,
And is absolved from all a heart must be;
All that it signed or chartered heretofore
Is cancelled now, the bankrupt heart is free;
So much of duty as you may require
Of shards and dust, this and no more of pain,
This and no more of hope, remorse, desire,
The heart once broken need support again.
How simple 'tis, and what a little sound
It makes in breaking, let the world attest:
It struggles, and it fails; the world goes round,
And the moon follows it. Heart in my breast,
'Tis half a year now since you broke in two;
The world's forgotten well, if the world knew.

LI

IF IN the years to come you should recall,
When faint at heart or fallen on hungry days,
Or full of griefs and little if at all
From them distracted by delights or praise;
When failing powers or good opinion lost
Have bowed your neck, should you recall to mind
How of all men I honoured you the most,
Holding you noblest among mortal-kind:
Might not my love—although the curving blade
From whose wide mowing none may hope to hide,
Me long ago below the frosts had laid—
Restore you somewhat to your former pride?
Indeed I think this memory, even then,
Must raise you high among the run of men.

LII

Oh, SLEEP forever in the Latmian cave,
Mortal Endymion, darling of the Moon!
Her silver garments by the senseless wave
Shouldered and dropped and on the shingle strewn,
Her fluttering hand against her forehead pressed,
Her scattered looks that trouble all the sky,
Her rapid footsteps running down the west—
Of all her altered state, oblivious lie!
Whom earthen you, by deathless lips adored,
Wild-eyed and stammering to the grasses thrust,
And deep into her crystal body poured
The hot and sorrowful sweetness of the dust:
Whereof she wanders mad, being all unfit
For mortal love, that might not die of it.

THE END